AF471869

God, Self and Ego

Discerning "Who's Who" on the Spiritual Journey

Doctoral project submitted to and accepted by the
Graduate Theological Foundation
Donaldson, IN USA

May 1996

by
Philip St. Romain, M.S., D. Min.
Contemplative Ministries, Inc.

Published on Lulu.com
March 19, 2010

ISBN: 978-0-557-37686-5

Introduction

I am happy to make this work available to the general public, as it has been downloaded many times from my website, shalomplace.com, through the years.. What follows is, essentially, the full text of my doctoral project, which was entitled *God, Self and Ego: An Exercise in Discernment.* It was written during the Fall of 1995, and accepted by my advisor and the staff of the Graduate Theological Foundation in Spring of 1996. When I let my publishers know of it, they expressed interest, but wanted a total rewrite to make it more palatable for a general audience. As I did not have the time nor inclination to do so, I put it up "as-is" in the Internet, for those who might be interested. Turns out, there seems to be a considerable interest in this topic, so here it is, the doctoral project, heavily footnoted, and somewhat "dense" or sketchy in places.

Ever since Vatican Council II, the metaphysical teachings of classical theologians like St. Thomas Aquinas have received short shrift. There are many reasons for this, none the least of which is the "pedagogical sins of the pre-Vatican II Church," as my friend Jim Arraj put it. Metaphysics was taught in seminaries and universities, but it was a dry and seemingly irrelevant topic. Following the Council, psychological approaches came more into vogue, and remain so today. But just how, precisely, do these approaches fit into a "larger understanding" of human nature?

It seems to me that without a metaphysical anthropology of some kind, it becomes very difficult to qualify the meaning of terms like God, Self and Ego. One need only read a few books on spirituality and mysticism to see just how differently these terms are used in the literature. For some writers, Ego is a false or illusory sense of individuality -- the primary obstacle to divine union. For others, Ego is natural and normal, though wounded and in need of healing. The classical writers of antiquity seem to use the term Self in the same way that modern writers use

Ego. Also, some writers, notably those with Eastern or New Age perspectives, use God and Self interchangeably. I think the theology and philosophy of St. Thomas Aquinas can help to bring clarity and focus to these terms.

This book was written with spiritual directors in mind, as the doctoral program I participated in was for a D. Min. in spiritual direction. I believe it's especially important for spiritual directors to have clarity concerning human nature and its relation to the divine, for it is precisely growth in such a relationship that we're hoping to support and encourage. But what would this entail? Should we be addressing the Ego-God, Self-God or Ego-Self-God approach? These different relationships aren't necessarily contradictory or mutually exclusive. Still, it helps to know what one is doing, and my hope is that the present work can help to sharpen one's focus in this regard.

Philip St. Romain
March 19, 2010

God, Self and Ego
Discerning "Who's Who" on the Spiritual Journey

Contents

God, Self and Ego
Discerning "Who's Who" on the Spiritual Journey

Part One: What is God, Self and Ego?

Since 1973, when my adult faith journey began, no issue has interested me more than the manner in which God and I are united. The reason for this interest has been personal as well as academic. Many times along the way, I have hurt myself because of distorted ideas about how God and I are united. There was a period, for example, in which I suffered greatly because of false humility. I actually believed that God loved me more if I put myself down, or considered other peoples' needs more important than my own. A number of traditional meditation manuals seemed to endorse this position in their contention that self-love is at the root of our sinfulness.[1] Then there was the Gospel mandate to deny self, pick up the cross, and follow Jesus.[2] All of this conspired to intensify an already bad case of low self-esteem and non-assertiveness. Thankfully, I came upon the writings of Fr. John Powell, S.J., who affirmed the value of a healthy self-love, thus enabling me to experience God's presence more fully as well.[3]

Among the many words today that are used in a variety of contexts—some of which are contradictory—none is so badly maligned as the word Self. Everyone uses the word at some

---

[1] One of my favorite devotionals was *The Imitation of Christ*, by Thomas a' Kempis, which I still believe to be a most valuable work. The reader will need to nuance the references to self, however. For example, in No. 40, we read, "Truly, I can well think and say: I am nothing and have no goodness of myself, but in all things I am of myself insufficient and tend to nothing." People with low self-worth already suffer enough from these kinds of convictions.

[2] Mark 8: 24.

[3] Especially helpful was *Fully Human, Fully Alive*.

time, and we all assume that we know what we mean by it. When pressed to define the term, however, we generally stammer, or else feel insulted for being asked to explain the obvious. Those of us who have, in addition, been exposed to the terminology of modern psychology will also encounter the term Ego, which is sometimes used to describe the Self of common parlance, but is frequently more nuanced. For most psychologists, Ego is not a disparaging term, but to the psychologically illiterate, it refers to fat-headedness. Who among us—even those familiar with psychological language—would like to be told that we were very Egoic?

Although most psychologists refer to the Ego as the conscious aspect of the Self, there is great variation among the schools of psychology concerning the relationship between Ego and Self. Some, like the Jungians, see the Ego as the conscious representative of a deeper Self.[4] Others do not delve into the metaphysical implications of their science, but focus primarily on helping the Ego adapt to its social situation. When encountering the writings of transpersonal psychologists, however, one finds many references to Self that sound similar to religious descriptions of God.[5] Transpersonalists also tend to regard the Ego as an illusory self, or a false self, thus contradicting the Jungian and even Freudian usage of the term.

As Christians come into increasing contact with Hindus, Buddhists, and Taoists, we find an even more confusing use of this terminology. For the Hindu, Self refers to the Atman, which is one with Brahman, the supreme God. Hence, the Hindu idea of Self is practically synonymous with the divine while the Ego is considered an illusory and provisional structure.[6] My first

---

[4] See "The Relations Between the Ego and the Unconscious," and "Aion: Phenomenology of the Self (The Ego, the Shadow, the Syzygy: Anima/Animus)" in *The Portable Jung*.

[5] A prime example of this can be found in "Personal and Transpersonal Growth: The Perspective of Psychosynthesis," by John Firman and James Vargiu in *Transpersonal Psychotherapies*.

[6] Writing in *The Complete, Illustrated Book of Yoga*, Swami Vishnu-devananda says about Self: "'I am indeed Brahman, or the Absolute,' without

impression when I met with this teaching was that it seemed to negate the dignity of individual life. My impression of the Buddhist teachings about Self was even more negative, for the higher grades of Buddhist mysticism speak of non-Atman, the loss of even the divine Self of the Hindu.[7] What could be left if even Self were lost, I wondered, to which the Buddhist reply is bliss, only bliss.

The encounter between Christian spirituality, modern psychology, and the religions of the far East challenges us to reexamine our understanding of human nature and its manner of union with the divine. One obvious step in the direction of discernment must be to clarify terminology in reference to God, Self, and Ego. If Christ says that self must go, and the Hindu says that Self must be realized, there seems to be an insurmountable contradiction between the goals of these two religions. But what does Christ mean by self, and what does the Hindu mean? Inter-religious dialogue has been attentive to these questions, but we still have a long way to go in formulating definitive responses.

---

difference, without change, and of the nature of reality, knowledge, and bliss. I am not the mind and the senses because the mind and senses are also instruments of the self. . . Therefore, the self is the witness of the body, mind, and senses, and because the self shines, the mind and senses reflect the light and appear as consciousness." Swami Vishnu-devananda, along with most transpersonal psychologists, views the Ego as the sense of personal identity derived from intellectual life. It is be worth noting that a number of influential Christian writers also use the word Ego in reference to an impermanent self, or even a false self. William Johnston speaks of Ego thus in *Being in Love*. Willigis Jaeger does the same in *Search for the Meaning of Life: Essays and Reflections on the Mystical Experience.*

[7] Many today tend to minimize the Buddhist experience by claiming that it refers to Ego-transcendence. Guatama knew what the Hindu meant by Atman, or True Self, however (see above footnote). When he speaks of non-Atman, he is referring to a new religious experience which was (perhaps) first realized by him. Roger Walsh, in "Phenomenological Mapping: A Method for Describing and Comparing States of Consciousness (*Journal of Transpersonal Psychology*). Vol. 27, No. 1, pp. 25-56, 1995)," provides a method for comparing different kinds of mystical states. The self sense of the Hindu is described as "unchanging transcendent Self," while the Buddhist "self sense is deconstructed into a changing flux: no-self."

This doctoral project will attempt to clarify the terminology concerning God, Self, and Ego. Given the contradictory usage of the terms God, Self, and Ego in the literature, I have little hope of arriving at a consensus definition. My only hope for establishing clarity is through usage of an understanding of human nature that is somewhat independent of the theological paradigms of the world religions. While transpersonal psychology proposes to give us such a picture, I believe it has thus far been overly influenced by writers who are clearly enamored with Hindu and Buddhist mysticism.[8] Therefore, I will look to philosophy, especially that of St. Thomas Aquinas and his explicators, to help clarify the terminology in question. On the whole, philosophers are also in conflict concerning the nature of human beings, but the philosophy of St. Thomas has stood the test of time better than any other. His philosophy is also compatible with a Christian view of life, which is an added plus for the spiritual director working out of a Christian tradition. As we shall see, his philosophy can even shed light on the religious experiences of Hindus and Buddhists as well. It is my hope that this reflection can assist Christian spiritual directors in helping their directees come to a clearer understanding of their own experiences of God and the manner in which God is calling them to union.

Essence and Existence

There are many starting points for doing philosophy. For purposes of this exercise in discernment, I shall begin with St. Thomas' observation of the two aspects of reality, namely essence and existence.[9] These observations are already developed in the Aristotelian tradition that he adapted, but he

[8] Perhaps the best-known, and most popular writer on transpersonal psychology is Ken Wilber, who has studied under the Yogi Da Love Ananda, and whose religious pathway is Buddhist. Wilber makes no secret of this in any of his works.

[9] For a deep, philosophical reflection on the Thomistic notion of essence and existence as worked out by Jacques Maritain, see Chapter 2 in Jim Arraj's scholarly work, *God, Zen, and The Intuition of Being*.

contributed his own insights unto a religious understanding of the matter.

Anything that can be conceived is an essence. Some essences, like Homer's idea of a Cyclops, exist only in our minds, while others, like a Blue Jay, also enjoy existence outside of our minds. The difference between a Cyclops and a Blue Jay is that the Blue Jay actually exists—it is a being—while the Cyclops does not. The philosophical concept of existence, then, tells us that something actually is, while the concept of essence tells us what something is. The Blue Jay experiences both aspects: it is, and, what it is is a Blue Jay. This is easy enough to understand.

Existence is obviously the larger concept: something that exists cannot be a what unless it is first a that. But what makes a *what* a what? Why is the Blue Jay a Blue Jay and not a Chickadee? Or, to use philosophical language, what is an essence?

The answer from the Thomists here is that "Essence is a certain capacity to exist. It stands in relation to existence as potency to act, and essence is the potentiality for a certain degree of existence."[10] A given essence, then, such as a Blue Jay, is a particular expression of an infinite number of possible existents.

The Thomists went on to describe a vast array of essences in terms of the strength of their being. Some essences, like those of chemicals, are weak in being because they can lose their distinctive form in merging with other chemicals. Other essences, like those of angels, are of such strength that each individual angel constitutes a whole species. A hierarchy of beings figures significantly in this philosophy, ranging from simple matter at the bottom to archangels at the top. No matter how strong the essence, however, it represents an expression of the potentiality of existence.

The concept of God may be defined as pure Existence and unlimited Essence. That God is and what God is are the same.

---

[10] *Ibid.*, p. 25.

If the essence of God was anything less, then God would also be a limited potentiality, which God is not. Creatures, on the other hand, do experience limitations in intelligence and freedom; God gives the creature its essence or being through an act, which is the gift of existence. Existence is not something a creature can control, nor deserve. The first, and greatest grace given to any creature is the fact *that it is*. We shall return to this affirmation several times during the course of this reflection.

Let's come up for air now, and put things in more simple language. What St. Thomas is saying is that everything that exists is given its uniqueness by something beyond itself, which is pure Existence, or God. What he is attempting to do, however, is not merely present this as an affirmation of religion, but as a conclusion which the very nature of reality suggests. Essence and existence might seem like mental concepts imposed by the mind on reality, but really they are not. "We are part of a world of existing things, existents, and our minds find in these existents the two dimensions of essence and existence. Essence and existence are found there because they are actually there. They are not merely intellectual constructs."[11] In his teaching on essence and existence, St. Thomas is describing one of the most basic intuitions of common sense.

As might be expected, this intuition of reality shows up in many other places as well. The Buddhist ideas of form and emptiness correspond to essence and existence, respectively.[12] So does the Taoist teaching on the Tao as the mother of the 10,000 things.[13] Islamic theologians have made use of Aristotle's

---

[11] *Ibid.*

[12] See D. T. Suzuki's provocative essay on "Knowledge and Innocence" in Thomas Merton's *Zen and the Birds of Appetite*.

[13] "The Tao that can be told is not the eternal Tao. The name that can be named is not the eternal name. The nameless is the beginning of heaven and earth. The named is the mother of the ten thousand things. Ever desireless, one can see the mystery. Ever desiring, one can see the manifestations. The two spring from the same source but differ in name; this appears as darkness. Darkness within darkness. The gate to all mystery."

philosophy to affirm the same relationship between God and creation. Indeed, it is truly amazing about that the Aristotelian-Thomistic teachings have fallen into disuse in these times. The reasons for this are many, and discussing them would take us far afield. Certainly, this is not the language or prevailing mind set of our times, but I do not find a better philosophy to have taken its place.

Emanantism and Creationism

In discussing the relationship between existence and essence, we have, for the moment, left ourselves open to a pantheistic understanding of creation. Pantheism means literally that God is all. Its view of essence is that it is an emanation of, or particularization of existence. Hence, essence is not a certain capacity to exist which a being possesses as its own, but an extension of existence in a particular form. This philosophy is widespread, predominating in the religions of the far East, and also finding expression among a number of Western thinkers.[14]

In its religious expression, emanationism maintains that God alone is real, and what we call the universe is naught but God expressing as the various forms we see about us. While this view might seem to affirm most powerfully the sacredness of creation, it also leads to gross violations of common sense when applied to the realm of identity, calling into question the validity of one's experience of being an entity distinct from other entities.[15] It is precisely this experience of individual identity that

---

(No. 1 of the *Tao te Ching*, by Lao Tse.)

[14] Western thinkers of a pantheistic bent would include Parmenides, Heraclitus, Paracelsus, Spinoza and Goethe. Philosophers and theologians from the Hindu tradition who have articulated a pantheistic view would include Shankara and Ramnuja. The common Buddhist notion that the world we see about us is a passing illusion, and only Absolute Mind is real constitutes a kind of a-cosmic pantheism.

[15] The Hindu Swami Rama writes, "Shakti (divine energy) is a projection of consciousness that veils the consciousness (Shiva) from which she was projected, in the innumerable illusory manifestations [Maya] that she brings forth and that we call the universe." (Brackets mine.) Quoted in "The

emantionists calls illusory. If only existence (or God) is real, then I (whatever that is) am not.

The implications of emanationism regarding one's understanding of God, Self, and Ego are obvious. If the sense of individual life is identified as Ego consciousness, then the Ego is nothing but an illusion. Why such an illusion should be so intensely and universally cherished is not explained to any great degree of intellectual satisfaction. Generally, the Ego is considered a provisional structure operating in the interest of personal survival. But just why, exactly, God should need an Ego to help God survive is an issue that seems not to provoke much reflection.

For the emanationist, it is Self, not Ego, that is the manifestation of God in human form. The Hindu calls this Self Atman, and sums up the relationship between Atman and the transcendent Brahman as "That Art Thou." That two different terms are used in reference to Self and God, here, is no contradiction of the emanationist position. Atman is the emanation of Brahman in human consciousness. The goal of Hindu spirituality is to lead one out of the illusory world (Maya) of the Ego to rest in the experience of Atman, or divine Self. In this experience, one comes to know pure being, knowledge, and bliss: sat-chit-ananda. Buddhism seems to work toward the same goal, only the theological language of Hinduism has been shed in favor of a more psycho-philosophical perspective.[16]

As Christians continue to encounter the religions of the far East through the many Hindus and Buddhists who have come West,

---

Awakening of Kundalini," from *Kundalini, Evolution and Enlightenment* (New York. Paragon House. 1979/90), John White, editor.

[16] As mentioned earlier, however, it may well be that the non- Atman, or no-self state of the Buddhism goes beyond the non- Ego state of Hinduism. Many writers, however, suggest that the Buddhist no-self and the Hindu Atman are both references to the same universal Self that underlies one's personal consciousness. For an insightful discussion of this topic, see *The Perennial Philosophy* (New York. Harper and Row. 1944.) by Aldous Huxley, pp. 1-11.

it is certain that these Eastern notions of God, Ego, and Self will challenge and, perhaps, confuse our own use of this terminology. Even if it were to be demonstrated that they use these words in reference to the same experiences that we use them, the emanationist/pantheist context suggests a different relationship among them than has been traditionally understood in the West. The philosophies and theologies that have inspired the development of Western culture are not emanationist/pantheistic, but creationist. At stake, here, is the manner in which the relationship between existence and essence is understood. This might seem a small matter, far removed from the real problems of life, but the consequences in terms of understanding one's true identity are monumental.

The creationist doctrine, which St. Thomas' philosophy supported, recognizes that essence is totally dependent upon existence for its being, but does not conclude from this that essence is identical to existence. Essence is a created thing—an expression of Existence, to be sure, but a being new and different from Existence.[17] In religious terms, we would say that the Being we call God creates beings who are entirely dependent upon God for their existence, but who are nonetheless beings distinct from God. The proof of this is that any created being is a form manifesting action, energy, freedom, and intelligence, but within limitations, whereas the Being synonymous with Existence itself knows no such limitations. Furthermore, the idea that God can become particularized into the many limited forms we see about us contradicts the concept of equivalency between God's essence

---

[17] In PtI, Q45 of *The Summa Theologia* St. Thomas Aquinas writes of "The Mode of Emanation of Things from the First Principle." His use of the word emanation is different from the emanationist position here discussed, describing, instead, the manner of procession of creatures from the Creator. Regarding the reality of a distinction between the creature and the Creator, St. Thomas writes: "Because creation is signified as a change, as was said above (I, 40, 2), and change is a kind of medium between the mover and the moved, therefore also creation is signified as a medium between the Creator and the creature. Nevertheless, passive creation is in the creature, and is a creature."

and existence. This concept, which is an affirmation of the simplicity of God—that God is indivisible into parts—is foundational in St. Thomas' understanding of essence and existence.[18] When pushed to the extreme, the emanationist view actually denies a distinction between existence and essence, while the creationist view maintains this distinction to be real and fundamental.

St. Thomas did not pretend to understand or explain precisely how God and creation are connected. This is a great mystery! His teaching on essence and existence describes something of the manner in which creation stands in relation to God. God and creation are two different entities, and yet the two are not separate. God is present in all of creation, and all creation has its being in God. This affirms the reality of an ever-present, ongoing union between God and the creature by virtue of the fact that the creature is constantly receiving its act of existence from God.[19] Some writers refer to this as a natural union, but I prefer the term existential union for obvious reasons. We shall say more about this type of union as we go along.

God and Self

If God's very Essence is pure Existence, then what is the essence of a human being? St. Thomas and those of his philosophical school spent a lot of time responding to this question. They considered the various kinds of beings observable on earth, and they reflected very deeply on the

---

[18] *Ibid.*, PtI, Q3 deals with the simplicity of God. In the Seventh Article, St. Thomas writes that . . ."there is neither composition of quantitative parts in God, since He is not a body; nor composition of form and matter; nor does His nature differ from His suppositum; nor His essence from His existence; neither is there in Him composition of genus and difference, nor of subject and accident. Therefore, it is clear that God is nowise composite, but is altogether simple."

[19] "God is in all things; not, indeed, as part of their essence, nor as an accident; but as an agent is present to that upon which it works. . .Therefore as long as a thing has being, God must be present to it, according to its mode of being." *Ibid.*, I, Q8, 1.

nature of pure spirits such as angels. The hierarchical universe which they described was divided into different levels of beings, which can be summarized as inanimate, vegetative, sensible, and spiritual. Each of four levels, in turn, evidenced differing grades of complexity.[20] Although the theory of evolution did not figure into their considerations, there is no reason to doubt that they would have accepted it as a partial explanation for these various grades of being—at least on the non- spiritual levels.

The human being is considered a spiritual being, sharing with the angels a capacity for rational intelligence, freedom, and self-possession. Unlike the angels, however, the human soul is fundamentally oriented toward matter; furthermore, the human soul incorporates the levels of vegetative and animal life. These levels exist in the human according to their unique powers, but all are in-formed by the spiritual soul so that they exist by means of the soul and for the soul.[21] For the Thomists, these lower levels were considered necessary to activate the spiritual intelligence of the soul. Without sensory information, which makes use of the lower three levels, the intelligence of the soul has nothing to act upon.[22] Once activated, however, the spiritual nature of human intelligence becomes manifest in its capacity for formulating abstract ideas several removes from sensory information, and in its capacity to make free choices.

Another important characteristic of the human essence is its corporate nature.[23] Because of its marriage with matter, Thomists consider the human soul to be lowest rung on the ladder of spiritual beings (see Figure One). This is not meant to denigrate the soul, only to say something of the strength of its being. Because pure spirits enjoy complete self-possession and

---

[20] For a good introduction to the Thomistic approach to levels of being, see Peter Kreft's *Angels (and Demons): What Do We Really Know About Them?.*
[21] *The Summa Theologia*, I, Q78, 1.
[22] *Ibid.*, I, Q82, 6.
[23] The term, corporate, is not meant to indicate that one soul belongs to many different people, for St. Thomas makes it quite clear that each individual possesses one soul. Corporate, here, refers to the fact that there are many souls representing the one, human species.

self-knowledge, St. Thomas concluded that each must be considered a whole species, for each summed up the possibilities available at its level of spiritual existence.[24] As we know from personal experience, the case is quite different for humans. None of us can claim complete self- possession and self-knowledge, and the reasons for this have more to do with the strength of our being, than with human sinfulness (which, no doubt, aggravates the matter). Neither does any one human represents all the possibilities of human existence; this belongs to the species as a whole.

The analysis of human nature given to us by the Thomists focuses primarily on humans in our objective existence. What about the subjective, interior implications of this view? It is not too difficult to draw a number of inferences from the Thomistic paradigm.[25]

All that was written about the soul can be applied to human consciousness, or Self. In considering the Self to be the essence of human interiority, we may affirm the following:

1. It is spiritual, encompassing the levels of animal, vegetable (physiological), and even inanimate being. This means that the the animal, vegetable, and inanimate realms of existence are present to Self through the vegetative (physiological), and sentient (animal, sensory) powers contained in the soul. This suggests a basis for the kind of cosmic consciousness described by so many mystics.

2. It is corporate, belonging to each individual as his or her own, but manifesting more fully in community. In this sense, Self is the medium in and through which humans know one another as human beings. It is the consciousness we share in common, and the primary basis for any possibility of empathy and understanding in relationships. Self-realization, then, implies Self-in-

---

[24] *The Summa Theologia*, I, Q75, 7.

[25] Human interiority is discussed by St. Thomas, but mostly in terms of intellectual life, rather than self-awareness.

relationship. Conversely, the more deeply one realizes Self as the root of one's Ego, the more deeply one finds union with other people. Far from being static (a criticism often directed against the Thomists' beings), Self is inherently social and relational.

3. As the essence of human interiority and subjectivity, Self is received directly from God in each moment.[26] Between God and Self, there is no obstacle to union. Looking toward God from this depth, Self knows God not as relational Partner, but as Source, Void, Emptiness, or Field of infinite possibilities. Self is "that" within us which is open to God, and which recognizes God.

4. The union between Self and God exists at every "point" at which God gives human existence. Hence, Self, and its union with God, is not confined to the heart, nor to the brain, but is to be found in every "place" where the human exists—including the physical body and its processes.[27]

This is indeed a very holistic conception of the Self!

Using the Thomistic model as the basis for this understanding of Self, we can now state with conviction that Self is an experience of the deepest subjectivity of a human being. It is also an experience of God insofar as God is immanent within Self. Self

---

[26] *The Summa Theologia*, I, Q90, 3: "Since, therefore, the rational soul cannot be produced by a change in matter, it cannot be produced, save immediately by God." So it is with the Self, who is the subject of the soul.

[27] *Ibid.*, I, Q76, 8: "But since the soul is united to the body as its form, it must necessarily be in the whole body, and in each part thereof." The same can be implied of Self if Self is held to be the subjective agent of the soul, and of God as the Giver of the soul. This is not to suggest, of course, that Self, nor its conscious Ego is aware the operations of the vegetable and animal levels. In describing the soul as the principle by means of which these levels operate in the human, St. Thomas did not imply that the intellect and its Self were cognizant of these operations. Indeed, the converse is more likely: that Self is present to the lower levels, and they are responsive to its operations. Some of the more outstanding yogic feats amply demonstrate the depth to which even autonomic responses can be made to respond to the influence of Self.

and God are not- one; they are two different entities. And yet Self and God are united by means of God's gift of existence in each moment. As one writer put it, "Self is God's habitat".[28] The implications of these reflections for leading people in spiritual direction should be obvious.

Self and Ego

In defining Self as the subjectivity of the human essence, we must also assert that Self is never found apart from individuals. Self tells us both that we are (an existent), and something about what we are: namely, human consciousness. Any further development of the human essence and its "what-ness" or "who-ness" must take place in the lives of individuals, who each reveal something of the face of Self. These insights suggest an explanation for our desire to become who we are—to realize our individual potentiality.

The term, Ego, is most frequently used in reference to the experience of individual, personal consciousness, and I accept this. In the present context, however, the Ego cannot be viewed as an illusory experience (although this can be said of the false self, which we shall consider shortly). Rather, Ego is considered here to be the individual, intentional agent of Self. The word intentional, here, means active and responsible.[29] Without the Ego, the potentiality of Self cannot be developed and expressed. Since it is natural for an essence to express its what-ness, we may conclude that it is natural for Self to manifest Egoically.

---

[28] This is stated several times in Dom Aelred Graham's delightful book, *Zen Catholicism*.

[29] St. Thomas writes that the "human intellect, which is the lowest in the order of intelligence and most remote from the perfection of the Divine intellect, is in potentiality with regard to things intelligible, and is at first like a clean tablet on which nothing is written (*The Summa Theologia*, I, Q79, 2)." Later, he writes of the necessity of an active intellect to extract from sensory information the forms bound up in matter (I, Q79, 3). What I am suggesting here is a similar relationship between Self and Ego.

Ego stands in relationship to Self as a sunbeam to the sun. They are not really two different entities, but neither are they the same experience of human subjectivity. The sun, here, represents Self as the vast potentiality of human consciousness which is always present to the Ego, but which is, for the most part, unconscious.[30] Like the sunbeam emanating from the sun, the Ego emanates from Self, having its root in Self, and its fundamental intention directed toward engagement in the outer world of other essences. Through this process of engagement and the experiences which ensue, the Ego forges its identity and its story. The "who I am" of Egoic consciousness is thus an ongoing process of discovery, with each experience revealing something new about one's giftedness and motives. This journey has been studied extensively by psychologists, who have, as a whole, given us a more or less coherent picture of the issues and stages in Ego-development.[31] Their analysis of the Ego-Self relationship is incoherent, however; sometimes it is even neglected. But, then, they are examining Ego-development in a far from perfect world, where the sunbeam has lost awareness of the sun from which it emanates.

We can speculate that, in a perfect world, the emanating Ego would nonetheless maintain awareness of its root in Self, and the God within and beyond.[32] Through its ongoing, realized union with Self as the source of its own subjectivity, the Ego would experience its unity with other people in Self, and its union with the cosmos through the lower levels of being present within Self. The holistic nature of Self would be also realized; no

---

[30] For Jung, the Self is the coordinating center of the unconscious mind, and also the totality of the psyche (see *Man and His Symbols*, pp. 161-162). The Ego is the conscious "agent" of the Self, but this does not imply that Self, as unconscious, is not an intelligence. Quite obviously, it is! Working from a Thomistic perspective, James Arraj, in *Mysticism, Metaphysics and Maritain*, devotes an entire chapter to the spiritual unconscious, which shares many features with what we are describing here as Self.

[31] See Jane Loevinger's *Ego Development*.

[32] In I, Q94, 1 of the *The Summa Theologia*, St. Thomas makes it clear that the first parents did not know God's Essence, for then they would have been unable to sin. Rather, they knew God through God's effects within and about themselves, and were not impeded by disorder within themselves.

internal splits would be experienced, no constriction of the Ego from the realm of the physical body. Something of the glory of God would be known through Self, and, if God so wished, an inter-subjective relationship between God and Ego could also exist. No dissolution or negation of Ego- intentionality would be required to experience this marvelous, unitive context of development. As long as the Ego maintained the same "attitude" as Self—open to God, the cosmos, social relationships, holistic experience—the identity and giftedness developed by the Ego would not contradict the unitive context. Indeed, Ego-consciousness would be the crowning glory of creation, Self, and God. Without an Ego-consciousness, there would be no one to appreciate the cosmos, no one to express Self, and no one (in this universe, at least) to praise God for it all.

The moral and spiritual implications of these reflections are many, the most important being the goodness of the individual and his or her developmental journey. It is good to be an Ego-consciousness, desiring to be, to grow, to develop our giftedness, and to share this with others. To the extent that we can do this in openness to God, social relationships, unity with the cosmos, and holistic living, we shall find our Ego experience most rich and meaningful. The problem, of course, is that this context for Ego-development has been lost, and, with it, the fullness of a healthy Egoic life.

The Ego and the False Self

The ideal relationship between Ego, Self and God described above is so drastically different from the common experience of most people that many would be inclined to believe that such harmony is only a theoretical affirmation. Unless we are quite advanced in the spiritual life, we experience Egoic consciousness in the context of insecurity, alienation, and judgmentalism. Indeed, so disordered is the Egoic experience that many writers on the spiritual life have concluded that the Ego itself is the cause of this disharmony. As we shall see, however, this view is unwarranted.

The problem for all of us is that Egoic development takes place in the context of conditional love. Why this is so does not interest the Buddhist, who maintains that even knowing the correct answer would not avail unto improvement. Reflection in the Judeo-Christian- Islamic tradition has led to the doctrine of Original Sin, in which a fall from innocence (and harmony) by our ancestors brought disorder to the whole race. The deep, fundamental unity of the human race was lost in some manner, and ever since then, a dynamic of fragmentation has been at work on both the individual and social levels.[33] Knowing about the doctrine of Original Sin can help us to understand the human plight, but the Buddhist is correct in pointing out that such understanding does not in itself bring liberation. We need a practical understanding of our disease: what it is, how it takes root, and how it is perpetuated. This understanding in itself contributes to its demise.

In an earlier work, I described the inflictions that accompany Ego development as follows:[34]

1. The environment in which we grow up loves us conditionally This begins in the womb, where the developing embryo is attuned to the emotional state of the mother, and, through her, to the rest of the world. Later, the care given the infant by the parents and family communicates conditional love in many ways.
2. When the embryo and later the infant is loved conditionally, he or she experiences at least a slight sense of rejection and the emotion of fear. If one is loved very little, there is great fear and distrust very deep within.
3. As the Ego begins to develop, the emotional consequences of conditional love—mostly fear, distrust, and shame—create a turmoil in our psychic energy which prevents the Ego from

[33] *Ibid.*, I, Q87, 1. Here, St. Thomas explains how the consequences of Original Sin result in disorder within a person, in human relationships, and in relationship with God.
[34] *Handbook for Spiritual Growth*, pp. 26-27.

developing in harmony with the Self. It as though the light of God mediated through the Self is blocked out by these turbulent emotions. Hence, the Ego will be much more attuned to the outside world and will be in some kind of avoidance posture toward the inner world of the unconscious as it develops.

4. The ideas and images of ourselves that we pick up from the developmental environment reinforce our feeling of being loved conditionally. In many ways, we learn that we are loved for what we do, not for who we are. At the level of thought, therefore, we conclude that we are conditionally lovable and acceptable. Our self-judgment and our perception of others' judgments of us—two integral parts of self-image—are deeply colored by this conditionality.
5. Concluding that we are only conditionally lovable and acceptable, we are constantly on the alert for the conditions by which we can become more acceptable to ourselves and others. These conditions are perceived to exist in externals—in the opinions of others, in accomplishments, in money and other possessions. The center of attention of the Ego, then, is drawn to the outside world as the source of happiness. 6. Having lost touch with the presence of God in the ground of our deepest Self, the Ego has also lost its true identity. To compensate, it identifies strongly with family roles, nation, race, athletic heroes, and other people to gain for itself some kind of identity through association.

There is much more that could be said about all this, but for purposes of the present discussion we note that the problem is not the existence of Ego, but its formation in the context of conditional love. A whole system of mental and emotional programming develops to cope with the fear, shame, distrust, and resentment which ensue from being loved conditionally. This system, not the Ego, is what goes by the name false self. Because it pervades the consciousness of the Ego, and many aspects of the unconscious as well, the false self system of programming needs to be understood if we are to become disentangled from it.

The six points listed above provide some of the key features of the false self. First, we note that it is a survival system developed to cope with the experience of conditional love. This in itself ought to tell us something about the antidote to it—namely, the perception of unconditional love. Secondly, we note that it directs the attention of the Ego to the outside world of essences at the expense of its attunement to the Self and God within. Furthermore, it reinforces this excessive attention to particularity through defense systems which not only keep us from experiencing our inner turmoil, but also prevent it from being healed. These defenses create splits—a face we show to the world, and a face that we hide most of the time. Thirdly, the key conviction of the false self is that we must do something to become loved and acceptable. This influences in the Ego an attitude of doing rather than being, of willful action instead of discerned responsiveness. Fourthly, the identity of the Ego is no longer naturally informed by Self, but is now structured largely by roles, identification, and judgments. The latter dynamic—comparing ourselves to others, pronouncing good and bad on people and situations—distorts the life of intellect and reason, further cutting off the Ego from the light of Self and emphasizing its sense of autonomy.[35]

The false self is thus a system of programming that reinforces itself at every turn, functioning more or less automatically in response to almost every situation that confronts us. Every time our decisions and behavior ensue from this programming, it becomes more deeply rooted within, and our ability to resist its influence is weakened. And, if that weren't enough to contend with, the entire culture we have developed with its many patterns of communication, mirror the false self system, providing social reinforcement of its dysfunction.

---

[35] There are many points of overlap between this psychological analysis of the consequences of Original Sin and St. Thomas', which emphasized weakness, malice, ignorance, and concupiscence (*The Summa Theologia*, I Q85, 1).

Pervasive and insidious though the false self may be, we know that it is not the whole of our experience of consciousness.[36] Something within even the worst of our species strains against it, and would be free of it completely if such a possibility seemed achievable. Such attainment is the concern of religion and, to a certain extent, psychology.[37] For purposes of this reflection, however, we must ask precisely what it is within us that resists and regrets the false self conditioning?

The response which suggests itself most strongly to me is that it is the Ego which strains against the false self. Although much of Egoic energy has become co-opted by the false self system, the Ego continues to emanate in every moment from its source in Self. As long as the tiniest spark of emanating Ego remains free, there is an individual consciousness available to do battle with the false self. The existence of this "remnant" of Egoic freedom and desire is implied in every religion, which would equip it with wisdom and connect it with Power to overcome the disharmony within. Grace builds on nature; this is a basic Thomistic conviction. Without an Ego, it would seem that grace would have nothing to work with, much less any-one to liberate.

From all of the above, we may conclude that the false self system of programing is not an existent being in the sense that the Ego-Self is. It is more like a computer virus which, once introduced into consciousness, perpetuates itself through decisions and behavior suggested by its fearful

---

[36] The Catholic view on Original Sin, which St. Thomas articulated in I, Q85, 1 (*Ibid.*), holds that "the natural inclination to virtue is diminished (not destroyed) by sin." In the Third Article of this Question, he writes that "sin cannot entirely take away from man the fact that he is a rational being, for then he would no longer be capable of sin. Wherefore it is not possible for this good of nature to be destroyed entirely." We may rightly conclude that the Ego as well, which is the subject of rationality, is not completely corrupted by sin.

[37] This point should not be minimized by religious people! Psychological disciplines can produce the fruit of greater self- knowledge and strengthen the Ego to make better choices. This does not get at the unconscious roots of the false self system, but without an empowered Ego, one will not get very far in the spiritual life.

judgmentalism.[38] To the extent that the Ego voluntarily cooperates with this programing, it "belongs" to the realm of the false self and (perhaps) to the evil spirits beyond. Even such cooperation would not lead to the conclusion that the Ego itself is depraved, or the obstacle to divine union, however. Given the goodness of Self as it is created in each moment, it would seem that at least some measure of freedom and intelligence would be available in the emanating Ego to resist the false self.[39]

It would also seem that the existence of the false self system is totally irreconcilable with an emantionists' view of the universe. If God is All, and God is pure Being, then why should God expressing in human form develop a false self? And to whom is the emanationist appealing when advancing a teaching on liberation if the very Ego being addressed is considered illusory? In a certain, morbid sense, then, the false self, or fallen human consciousness, proves the creationists' view by implying a misuse of freedom in a being who is not God (unless, of course, we deny the reality of sin, or else consider God to be capable of sin). The creationist also speaks to the dignity of that freedom by inviting the Ego to become committed to another way of life.

Summary

So, what is Self and Ego?

Put simply, it is "I".

But this ineffable experience we know to be "I" has two aspects: potentiality and actuality. The "I" of potentiality is the larger,

---

[38] Questions 86 and 87 in Part I of *The Summma Theologia* reflect on how sin brings darkness into the soul, and how one sin can lead to another—until the Light of grace cleanses the soul, that is.

[39] Although St. Thomas and many, many others have written about mortal sins which destroy "the principle of the order whereby man's will is subject to God" (Ibid. I, Q87, 3), they also recognize the possibility of repentance from such sins. This possibility, it would seem, presupposes the existence of some measure of freedom and intelligence.

more universal aspect; the individual actualization of this potential is more unique and personal. Hence, Self can be considered the subject of the unconscious, and Ego the subject of desire, intellectual activity, and conscious experience. These are not two different subjects, but they are two different experiences of "I". Self is "I" as the human spirit, who is present in desire and all manner of experiences, while Ego is the conscious and active dimension of "I" in this embodied state. When one consciously realizes this connection between Self and Ego, then the Ego loses its sense of alienation and isolation and begins to experience the social, cosmic, transcendent and holistic qualities of Self.

Because of our false self conditioning, however, our awareness of this connection between Self in Ego can be so terribly distorted that the Egoic "I" does not know from whence it comes, and so it attaches to all manner of things within and without the person in an attempt to complete itself. "I" can then become lost in the convoluted activities of the mind and emotions, becoming, instead, a "me," or object of my own mental activity. In such cases (and they are legion), then "I" am not merely shaped by my experiences, but determined by them. They are not "mine," but "me." Excessive self-definition and judgmentalism follow from the creation of this mind- self, which is not-"I".

And what of God? Is God "I"?

No, God is not "I". Rather, God is the "Am" in which "I" affirm the fact of my existence: "I Am." This "Am", or pure Being, is utterly distinct from "I", for "I" cannot, of its own accord, know anything more about It than the fact that "It Is." And yet Being is also the source of "I"; apart from It, "I" has no existence, no "Am." Something of Existence must therefore be present within "I", for It is the means by which "I" has its own being. "I" cannot extract Existence from itself, however, so "I" can never know what it is apart from Existence. Through the "I" in every person, then, something of the glory and numinosity of Existence Itself shines forth. Those who are awake to their own "I" know this truth, but those who have lost themselves in the disordered mental activity stirred up by the false self are asleep to the wonder of Existence.

Part Two

Facilitating Unitive Experiences

Following up on the reflections in Part One, it is possible to identify several kinds of unitive experiences:[40]

1. *Ego-false self.* This is not a union between two entities, but an infection of Ego by a system of conditioning which propagates itself whenever one acts according to its suggestions. In this sense, the false self-Ego relationship is very much like that which exists between cancer cells and the body.

2. *Ego-Self.* Although the Ego is the conscious agent of the Self, and therefore not something essentially different from Self, we can speak of a relationship between Ego and Self that may indeed be facilitated in spiritual direction. Because of the disordering influence of the false self, the Ego has lost awareness of its connection with Self, and so it must work to recover this awareness.

3. *Ego-God.* The Ego and God are two different entities, and a wide variety of relationships between them is possible through the various powers of the soul in which the Ego operates. Thus one we can recognize an Ego-God relationship mediated through the imagination, the intellect, the emotions, the desires, and even the body. Every Ego-God relationship is also colored by the many experiences with which the Ego is identified, as well as the false self system which influences Egoic life.

4. *Self-God.* The Ego-God relationship involves Self insofar as Self is the very subjectivity of the Ego, but what is referred to here is the union which exists deep within between God and

---

[40] My use of the term "unitive" is much broader here than is the classical Catholic stages of the spiritual life, where the "unitive way" refers to a deep and abiding union between God and a person.

Self. This union cannot be fully known or experienced unless the Ego is either transcended or regressed.

5. Ego-Self-God. This union would include elements of no. 3 and 4 described above.

During the process of spiritual direction, issues pertaining to one or more of these types of union will predominate at any given time. Even if one regards the Ego-Self-God union as the goal toward which spiritual direction in the Christian religion moves, it is most unlikely that the different facets of this experience will be developed at the time and the same rate. Sometimes, Ego-God issues will prevail, and at others, the Ego-Self connection will require attention. Nor should one conclude that these types of union are mutually exclusive. For example, growth in the Ego-God relationship can certainly stimulate the Ego-Self relationship. Therefore, the spiritual director would do well to be cognizant of these different types of union and the issues related to each. In doing so, the director will truly be a co-discerner of how the Spirit is working in the lives of his or her directees.

Facilitating Ego Authenticity

The practice of authenticity incorporates the virtues of honesty, self-knowledge, acceptance, and humility. Its goal is to help the Ego do what it must to break free of the phoniness and reliance on externals caused by the false self system. By practicing disciplines which promote authenticity, the Ego comes to "feel what it feels and know what it knows;"[41] it becomes connected with its own experiences, and more in touch with its story. This might involve experiencing unpleasant emotions and attitudes, or admitting shortcomings that had previously been denied. Inauthenticity arises in large part from one's unwillingness to face these negative aspects of interiority. Therefore, when

---

[41] This is a phrase used by Anne Wilson Schaef in many of her books to describe a healthy person, in contrast to one who is codependent. See *Co-Dependence: Misunderstood, Mistreated.*

negativity is encountered, it must be acknowledged in a spirit of honesty and self-acceptance, rather than self-condemnation. But there is more than negativity to be found within; pleasant emotions and access to one's own inner wisdom also come with this practice.

The practice of authenticity is foundational to the different kinds of union mentioned above. It facilitates a differentiation between the true Ego and the false self conditioning; it is required in the Ego-God relationship; and it is an essential prerequisite to knowing the deeper subjectivity of the Self. The Christian spiritual life has as its goal something far more wonderful than the authentic Ego, of course, but without this effort on the part of human nature, there is nothing for the grace of the Spirit to perfect.

There are many ways to facilitate Ego authenticity, some of which have their roots more in existential philosophy and psychology than in the Christian tradition proper. The Twelve Step recovery process also includes many practices which serve this goal quite effectively. Listed below are a few examples of disciplines which promote authenticity:

1. Encouraging the directee to ask him/herself often:
   a. How do I feel about this situation?
   b. What do I think/believe about . . . (whatever)?
   c. What do I want?
   d. What are my motives?
   e. Am I relating?

2. Journaling/diary reflection at the end of each day, using the questions in no. 1 to look at specific situations from the day. Formal approaches to journaling are also taught at workshops and retreats, and these can also be helpful.[42]

---

[42] For example, the Progoff approach, which is taught in many retreat centers.

3. Deliberately making the effort to refrain from saying or doing what is inauthentic. Practicing honesty in speech.

4. Working the Twelve Steps of recovery groups, especially Steps One, Four, Six, Eight and Ten.[43]

- Step One: "Admitted we were powerless over (alcohol, drugs, sex, shopping, work, worrying, controlling others, etc.), that our lives had become unmanageable."
- Step Four: "We made a searching and fearless moral inventory of ourselves."
- Step Six: "We were entirely ready to have God remove our defects of character."
- d. Step Eight: "We made a list of all persons we had harmed, and became willing to make amends to them all."
  e. Step Ten: "We continued to take inventory, and promptly admitted it when we were wrong."

5. Learning communication skills which facilitate more accurate and honest expression of feelings and expectations in relationships.[44]

6. Acting according to one's own beliefs, and not according to shoulds, musts, and oughts imposed by others in the name of authority—unless one chooses to act in such manner out of charity.

7. Making use of various resources for understanding one's personality and giftedness.[45]

---

[43] The proliferation of resources for working the Twelve Steps has been an invaluable aid for many in recovery programs, or who simply wish to use the Steps as a way to grow. See, for example, *The Twelve Steps: A Spiritual Journey* and my own book, *Twelve Steps To Spiritual Wholeness: A Christian Pathway*. Liguori Publications. 1992).

[44] An excellent resource is *Will the Real Me Please Stand Up: 25 Guidelines for Good Communication*, by John Powell, S.J. Also relevant is one of my books, *Lessons in Loving: Developing Relationship Skills*.

[45] For work with Jung's psychological types and Sheldon's body and temperament types, I recommend James and Tyra Arraj's highly readable book, *Tracking the Elusive Human*. Workshops and retreats on Jung's

8. Committing oneself to an ongoing process of education, personal growth, and self-examination.

This last discipline is especially important, pointing out that authenticity is an ongoing practice, not a permanent achievement. The more one begins to think, feel, and act authentically, the greater the likelihood that authentic living will prevail in the future. A likelihood is not a guarantee, however. Because of the incredible pervasiveness of false self conditioning in each of us, inauthenticity can be reasserted at any time. Constant awareness and vigilance are required!

Of course, it goes without saying that what's good for the directee is also required for the director. Only the director with a relatively authentic Ego can recognize the same, or its absence in others. In either case, I believe it is important for the director to stress the importance of this value in the first session, and frequently thereafter. Complete honesty from the directee might not be forthcoming until a requisite level of trust is attained. The more authentic the director, however, the more likely will be the development of an atmosphere of openness, acceptance, and honesty.

Ego-God Relationship

From the standpoint of the Ego-false self, God is totally transcendent, or external to the Ego. The means by which God is "drawn" to attend to the needs and desires of the Ego is through various kinds of good works, the more religious of which are considered especially efficacious. God is viewed as One who can help this disordered Ego obtain its wants, and the Ego considers itself to be one who can help God accomplish what God wishes. Between the two entities, there is a covenant based on mutual self-interest. Prayer is thus mostly petitionary, and religious involvement serves to reinforce one of the Ego's

---

psychological types, the Enneagram, family of origin roles, and other means for self-understanding are offered at retreat centers throughout the country.

identifications as Christian, Catholic, etc. If God is not forthcoming with answers to prayers, however, then the Ego questions God's goodness and justice, perhaps going so far as to break off its formal religious affiliation, or to stop praying altogether. Such, alas, is the case with millions and millions of souls, who know nothing of God, and who are trapped in their own conditioning.

The experience of God by the Ego striving for authenticity is different, but it is not totally devoid of the attitude of entitlement as long as any vestige of the false self remains.[46] The authentic Ego is capable of experiencing God as both transcendent Other, and as a Presence immanent in its own subjectivity. In both cases, however, the context of union is inter-subjective, the Egoic "I" relating itself to the divine "Thou," and receiving, at times, a sense that the divine is communicating with it in return. Because God cannot be directly encountered through the senses, as is the case with other people, the Ego must find another way to open itself to the divine. This openness and receptivity must therefore take place in the more spiritual powers of the soul, especially the intellect and the will. It is here that the assents of belief and trust in God produce the virtue of faith. Without such faith, God cannot be known by the Ego.[47]

Facilitating the Ego-God relationship in spiritual direction calls for considerable attention to the issues of belief in God, and trust in God. What are the directee's images and concepts of God? How do these encourage or discourage entrusting one's life to God? These questions can provide a focus for invaluable dialogue between the director and directee. It is appropriate in such discussions for the director to prod and probe for more detailed descriptions of the images of God to which the directee

---

[46] According to Fr. Thomas Keating in *Invitation to Love: The Way of Christian Contemplation*, we are never totally free of the false self in this life, but increasing freedom is experienced as one undergoes the purifications of the dark nights of the soul.

[47] For an excellent reflection on faith using Thomistic and other approaches, see James Arraj's *The Inner Nature of Faith: A Mysterious Knowledge Coming Through the Heart.*

is attached. To help the directee move toward a more mature understanding of God, the director should share his or her own images, and recommend reading and other resources (12 Step work, classes, videos, etc.). Although this aspect of spiritual direction might seem to be overly focused on religious education, it nonetheless has its place in a relationship of spiritual direction. To the extent that dysfunctional images of God are held by the directee, growth in the Ego-God relationship will be inhibited.

The issue of trust in God is closely connected with one's image of God. The surrender of the will to the care of God's Spirit cannot take place to any depth as long as the God to Whom one is surrendering is perceived as capricious in love and acceptance. More than likely, too, issues concerning trust in human relationships influence the level of trust and surrender which the directee is able to offer to God. Within this context, it is appropriate for the director to inquire about how trust is experienced in relationships with others. Where unresolved hurt and resentment in human relationships are impeding trustful surrender to God, the director should call attention to this, and recommend some process for coming to forgiveness and reconciliation. Twelve Step work, the Sacrament of Reconciliation, and psychotherapy can be helpful unto this end.

At this point, it needs be said that the Christian tradition has enormous wisdom and resources for facilitating the faith relationship between God and the Ego. Above all else, what is emphasized is that the Ego look beyond itself to God—to love God for God's own sake, rather than any benefits which might accrue to the Ego.[48] Several practices most strongly emphasized in the tradition are listed below:

---

[48] Consider the words of the Sufi woman-saint, Rabi'a. "God, if I worship Thee in fear of hell, burn me in hell. And if I worship Thee in hope of Paradise, exclude me from Paradise; but if I worship Thee for Thine own sake, withhold not Thine everlasting Beauty."

1. *Ethical behavior.* The Ego personality must make a deliberate effort to conform its will and energy with the will of God, as understood in terms of Love. The practice of virtue is especially recommended to counteract the selfish tendencies of the false self system. Through constant effort, the virtues become more habitual, enabling one's conscience to become more at peace, and the Ego more open to a deeper relationship with God.
2. *Prayer.* This is the primary way in which faith as relationship with God is deepened. Generally, the Ego begins with active forms of prayer like reading and reflecting on Scripture, affective prayer of petition, thanksgiving, and remorse, or even prayer using the imagination. In Christianity, the relationship between God and Ego is focused primarily in the person of Jesus Christ, who is the friend of all Egos, and a human partner in dialogue. Through ongoing faithful, committed dialogue with Christ in prayer, the Ego begins to sense its connection with God in deeper realms, which transcend the usual activities of the mind. This is the beginning of contemplative prayer.
3. *Ritual.* As an enactment of some aspect of myth, ritual serves to help the Ego experience the larger, communal dimension of its relationship with God. The Ego-God story can easily become a privatized, a-historical journey without ritual or some other form of communal worship. Traditionally, of course, the Sunday service or Eucharist has served this purpose in Christianity.

Many Christians who enter spiritual direction have already been exposed to rituals and ethical teachings, of course; some have also been active in prayer as well. Their experiences in these three areas have not always been fruitful, however, which is precisely why some are coming to see a spiritual director. Again, it is fruitful to explore what their past experiences have been. What are their beliefs about ethical behavior? Do they know that there is more to Christian ethical behavior than sexual responsibility? What has prayer been like for them? And what have been their experiences with ritual? Eventually, the directee must come to see that ethical behavior, prayer, and ritual are indispensable for growing in relationship with God. If these have not been meaningful experiences in the past, however, the director will need to be especially discerning in suggesting that they be given another try. It is my view that the best place to start is with prayer, for that is the area that most directees are willing to explore more deeply. If they can begin to experience a connection with God in prayer, then encouragements unto ethical living and community involvement will come more easily. Where the commitment to prayer is lacking, it is very difficult to facilitate ongoing relationship with God.

The Ego-God relationship described above is highly interpersonal and relational. This need not be the only way in which the Ego feels its way toward God, however. Another, somewhat impersonal way for the Ego to come to God is through intuition of being. This is a more metaphysical, or philosophical approach, in which one comes to the intuitive realization that one's own existence, and also that of other things, is a participation in pure Existence Itself. Jacques Maritain described two dispositions for coming to this intuition.

The first is a sensitivity to the actual existing world around us. This means an immersion in the concrete world of things by means of our senses, for through them we have a "blind existential perception' of the mystery of existence. . . The second necessary disposition for attaining this intuition is to be still enough to listen to the mystery of being that is whispered by all things. This intuition demands, not intricate intellectual technique, but rather an 'active attentive silence' and a 'degree of intellectual purification' by 'which we become sufficiently disengaged, sufficiently empty to hear what all things whisper and to listen instead of composing answers."[49]

Jim Arraj describes several exercises to cultivate the intuition of being. The most concise is direct examination of the statement, "I am."

---

[49] *God, Zen, and the Intuition of Being*, pp. 38-39.

> How simple this 'I am' appears, but what really is this 'I'? We are convinced we know, since we live with our 'I' in such intimate terms, but the foundation for the true meaning of the 'I' is not simply the 'I' itself but it is the 'am'. The 'I' is an expression, a contraction, of the 'am', but do we know what this 'am' is? . . . If we question the 'I' in the light of 'am', it can lead us to an abyss where the very meaning of our 'I' seems to crumble and we grow afraid that our 'I' is dissolving and there is nothing beyond it.[50]

Thus does the Ego come to stand before the mystery of God, Who is known here not so much as a relational partner, but as the Source of one's own being. The Ego that emerges from this encounter becomes radically purified of its identifications with roles and labels, and more firmly established in its true center, who is God.

Coming to God through cultivation of the intuition of being is a practice hardly known or encouraged by Christian spiritual directors. This "way" seems to make little use of faith as it has been traditionally understood, but there need not be a conflict between faith and the intuition of being. In fact, the intuition of being is a way soundly rooted in the philosophy of St. Thomas Aquinas.[51] Through Christian faith, one can develop the interpersonal aspects of the Ego-God relationship, and through the intuition of being, one can be led to a different experience of the mystery of God. The same Ego and the same God are involved in both experiences, to be sure, but the nature of the encounter is different. In many ways, the intuition of being can help to purge the Ego of false attachments far more rapidly than some of the more traditional, ketaphatic approaches, which tend to make use of anthropomorphic projections concerning the nature of God. These projections unwittingly serve to reinforce the Ego in its narrow structures of identity, thus closing it off to a deeper, more authentic encounter with the God of mystery.

---

[50] *Ibid.*, pp. 85-86.
[51] *Ibid.*, p. 36.

Theological justifications for the Ego-God relationship are soundly rooted in the Scripture, and in the constant teaching of the Church. Christ has come not only to save the species as a whole, but also every individual who belong to the species. The most powerful image of this is Christ the good shepherd, who actively seeks out the lost to bring them into the community of salvation.[52] In Christ, God is revealed as the Beloved of the Ego, who calls us to relationship and heals the Ego of its infection by the false self. This is accomplished in time through the action of his Spirit, working in the whole psyche to re-center the Ego in God and enable it to share in Christ's own consciousness of God. The traditional accounts of dark nights of the soul and purification processes describe something of how the Ego is healed of the false self and integrated into Christ.[53] In the end, everything proper to Ego consciousness is preserved, and the Ego is enabled to participate directly in the consciousness of Christ himself. The Ego comes to know even as it is known. Furthermore, it knows with the knowing of the One by whom it is known.[54] This "Christian enlightenment" can be tasted even in this life. It is the destiny of all who allow themselves to be found and pastured by the Good Shepherd.

Ego-Self Relationship

Several times during the course of this work, we have noted that the Ego and the Self are not separate, but are nonetheless different aspects of human subjectivity. The Ego is one's personal, individual consciousness, and Self is the deeper, more universal human consciousness.

One of the consequences of the false self infection of Ego is the loss of the experience of an Ego-Self connection. In almost everyone, the false self Ego is developed to such an extent that the sense of individual consciousness predominates over the

---

[52] John 10: 11-18.

[53] See *Invitation to Love*, chapters 10-16.

[54] This knowing is a very real experience of the beatific vision, which will become perfectly established after death.

deeper sense of Self. In terms of the philosophical paradigm sketched in Part I, we might say that the false-self Ego is more attuned to the "whatness" of things and the world of particularity than it is to the "thatness" of things and their deep, fundamental unity. We are more aware of separateness than union, and so we feel isolated, or cut off from other people and creation. Growth in Ego authenticity and in the Ego-God connection can help to restore the Ego-Self connection, but more direct, intentional disciplines which move in this direction can also be used. Indeed, intentional work on the Ego- Self relationship has been far too neglected in many schools of spiritual direction—in this writer's opinion, at least.

Before mentioning practices which can promote growth in the Ego- Self connection, it might be helpful to some directors to note the spiritual significance of this work. First, we note that any movement of the false self Ego from its attachment to the world of particularity is potentially beneficial. God is not a particularity, and so the Ego must eventually give up looking for God in the same way that it looks at other people and the world. Second, the Ego who realizes its rooting in Self knows itself to be both an individual consciousness and a member of the human family. This gives rise to a new way of seeing others; me-and-you consciousness co-exists with we-consciousness. Empathy, compassion, and community are enhanced through growth in the Ego-Self connection. This is very good! Finally, it was mentioned earlier that Self is the habitat of God in each person. Another author has noted that Self is that within us which recognizes God.[55] To be awake at this level, then, can only deepen one's awareness of God.

There are several kinds of disciplines which can enhance realization of the Ego-Self connection. Recalling the basic "attitudes" of Self discussed in Part I, we now recognize that the Ego must also embrace these attitudes if it is to be the

---

[55] Ann Belford Ulanov, writing in *The Fires of Desire: Erotic Energies and the Spiritual Quest*, page 160.

conscious agent of Self, rather than the slave of its false conditioning.

1. *Openness to Transcendence.* The Ego must come to recognize that its existence is received from a Source greater than itself. The disciplines discussed in the above section on the Ego-God connection can help the Ego regain its orientation toward Transcendence.
2. *Social Orientation.* The Ego must make an effort to become part of a community, as was also noted above. Simple things like fulfilling one's social obligations, community service, keeping up with the news of the world, praying for the needs of others, and loving someone else as fully as possible can help to open the Ego to a larger experience of life.
3. *Cosmic Orientation.* Self is fundamentally open to the cosmos, but most people today have lost their sense of connection with Nature. The technological culture in which we live is partly responsible for this, but we can make choices to remedy some of the damage. Taking walks, sitting outside, bird-watching, camping, fishing, hunting, watching sunsets, swimming in the ocean—these and many other activities help to reawaken in us a sense that we are part of a world that is larger than our Ego desires. This has been a missing piece in many approaches to spiritual growth, for the practices mentioned here do not seem very religious. Perhaps one of the reasons so many have become attracted to New Age and Eastern practices, however, is because they seem to appreciate the cosmic and ecological dimension of spirituality more-so than the spiritualities of the West have done—at least until recently.
4. *Holistic Orientation.* The false self Ego is a constriction of consciousness away from wholeness and polymorphous sensuality; genital sensuality and intellectual consciousness predominate instead. The consequence is that most people are out of touch with their bodies and their emotions, except when they eat, drink, have sex, or when they suffer. Increasing contact with Nature can help to restore a sense of wholeness, but a great deal more will be required of many. The recovery of the body calls for proper diet, exercise and

sleep. The recovery of emotional life is much more difficult, for most people have repressed many unpleasant emotions, and these will eventually come into awareness when the mechanisms of repression are loosened on the spiritual journey. Practices such as journaling and healthy communication skills can be helpful. In many cases, therapy and a support group will also be required.

In the context of developing the holistic dimension of the Ego-Self connection, I see the psychology of C. G. Jung as providing invaluable tools and wisdom. Jung's approach entails a deliberate encounter between the Ego and the unconscious through the medium of dream material, active imagination, and by exploring one's psychological type. The goal is to encounter the various opposing energies in the unconscious and to eventually reconcile them in a higher synthesis between the Ego and the unconscious. In this manner is the deeper potentiality of the Self realized and the union between Ego and Self made conscious. Happily, many spiritual directors are making use of Jung's psychology in their work with directees.[56]

There is one additional "method" for awakening the Ego-Self connection, and it is perhaps the most common and effective means of all. I am speaking here of the role of suffering in human life. The truth is that most people will not become too terribly interested in developing the attitudes discussed above through the practices recommended until their former manner of living no longer works for them. In the retreat center where I work, the majority of people who attend our programs have recently experienced a loss, or they are trying to recover from an addiction of some kind. After they get a taste of healthy spirituality, they might continue to come for different reasons, but that is not how they start out. The consequence for living in the false self Ego is suffering, as Buddha noted 2,500 years

---

[56] For an excellent reflection on Jung's psychology and Christian spirituality, see Jim Arraj's *Jungian and Catholic? The Promises and Problems of the Jungian-Christian Dialogue*.

ago.[57] This suffering, or cross, is the hammer and chisel which cracks the hard shell of the false self Ego, enabling the restoration of a connection between the Ego and God in Self. It is for this reason that the cross is the symbol of Christianity,[58] and the director ought to help the directee understand the purpose of his or her suffering as part of the process of rebirth. Suffering that can be perceived as meaningful is much easier to bear than meaningless pain, which leads to despair. Of course, the issue of meaninglessness is closely related to lack of faith in God, and so the relationship between suffering and faith can be a fruitful area for the director and directee to explore together. Christ said that if we wish to find ourselves (the true Self, that is) we must pick up our crosses daily and follow him. This is the long, hard work of the spiritual life—a work that can be assisted, however, through all the kinds of practices described in the above sections.

Self-God Relationship

The philosophical model discussed in Part I of this work has affirmed the existence of a deeper, more universal level of human consciousness that underlies and gives rise to Egoic consciousness. We called this Self. To experience this consciousness directly, Egoic consciousness would have to be set aside, or even deconstructed for a period of time. At this point, many would ask if such a direct experience of Self possible, or, if so, desirable?

The answer to both questions is "yes." It is possible to experience Self without Ego, and there are many positive outcomes ensuing from this experience. There are also pitfalls and dangers, such as the awakening of powerful energies in the unconscious, or the emergence of psychic gifts that one might not be prepared to deal with.

---

[57] Buddhist spirituality begins with the recognition that life is suffering, and that the root of suffering is desire—understood, here, as the desires which ensue from the false self. 19. 1 Cor. 1: 17-25.

[58] 1 Cor. 1: 17-25.

Facilitating direct experiences of the Self-God relationship has not been a part of spiritual direction in the Christian tradition, however. The only clear examples of this experience in Christianity that comes to mind are the ecstatic experiences of Christian contemplatives, and these are not sought directly.[59] Nevertheless, they are not as rare as one might expect. Three directees who visit with me regularly—all lay people with ordinary lives—have shared with me on many occasions that there are times in prayer when they experience something akin to sleep. I myself have experienced this as well. One is not actually sleeping, but the level of absorption in prayer is such that the operations of the senses and intellect are virtually silenced. There is no waking awareness, no sense of time, and no slouching of the posture (as during sleep). When the intensity of absorption subsides and there is a return to sensory awareness, a profound sense of the unity of all things in God prevails. For a few minutes—sometimes longer—this sense of unity eclipses Egoic consciousness; there is no awareness of an individual self separate from God and creation. One knows as experiential truth that we are all part of God and one another. This is the direct experience of the Self-God relationship, and it is very good! In its pure state, the experience is short-lived, but the Egoic consciousness which returns (as it must) has been significantly contextualized by the ecstatic experience. The world of separate things perceived by the Ego is known in the context of unity, the Ego- Self bond has been purified, and the Ego-God relationship strengthened. Henceforth, the Ego can "tune in," as it were, to the consciousness of Self by simply shifting its awareness from the perception of separate things to the realization of unity.

---

[59] Antonio Royo, O.P. and Jordan Aumann, O.P. describe ecstatic prayer as "a gentle and progressive swooning which terminates in the complete alienation of the senses. Although the ecstatic person does not see or hear or feel anything, it is evident that the individual is neither deal nor asleep. Usually the expression on the fact of the individual is radiant, as if the person has been transported to another world." *The Theology of Christian Perfection*, page 551.

Coming to experience the Self-God union through contemplative ecstasy begins with an Ego-God involvement through prayer. As the Ego is drawn closer to God, it is eventually brought to the "place" within where God is closest to the Ego—the Self. By surrendering itself to God in love, the sense of separateness that is the Ego's native state is transcended as the Ego enters into the unitive embrace between Self and God. The cosmic, social, transcendent, and holistic aspects of Self are experienced directly, leaving the Ego that returns to the world of space and time with a new perspective on reality. Throughout this experience, however, the Ego is never repressed, regressed, or deconstructed. Rather, its ordinary manner of knowing is transcended as it is drawn to the consciousness of Self, in which the unity of all things in God prevails over the perception of separateness.

The way of Ego-transcendence in ecstatic absorption in God is the predominant Christian pathway to the direct experience of the Self-God union. There are other pathways to this experience, however. All require, at least initially, the cooperation and direction of the Ego. Eventually, however, the ordinary functioning of the Ego is frustrated by the very methods which the Ego has undertaken. The three essential characteristics of some of these disciplines are as follows:

1. *Reducing the flow of sensory information.* The body may be calmed through yogic stretches; meditation proceeds in a quiet environment; the eyes are closed; a posture is assumed which minimizes bodily distractions.[60]
2. *Reducing the activity of the intellect.* Attention may be directed to the breath; a mantra may be repeated when distracting thoughts emerge; one observes distractions "from a distance," without becoming involved in them;

[60] When withdrawn from the senses, the soul "is then nearer to the spiritual world, and freer from external distractions." *The Summa Theologia*, I, Q86, 4.

counting breaths also frustrates intellectual activity, as does using a koan.[61]

3. *Reducing the movement of the will to a state of desirelessness.* The disciplines above contribute to this somewhat, but more important is the ongoing practice of non-attachment to the things and experiences of this world. If the will must be given any "goal," it is to be lovingly present to the moment, with no strings attached. The purpose of meditation is to do nothing more, nor less, than growing in this presence.[62]

When deprived of sensory information, the desire for something in particular, and the activities of imagination and reasoning, consciousness loses its Egoic form. We might say that, in such cases, the Ego is deliberately de-constructed by eliminating from consciousness the mechanisms that make Egoic life possible. What is left when Egoic consciousness is thus "subtracted" from the psyche? The answer is obviously the deeper, more universal realm of consciousness from which the Ego is derived: namely, Self.[63] This may be experienced directly in various levels of intensity that deepen over time. Psychic gifts and upheavals of energy from the unconscious might also be awakened as a consequence of these experiences. As more Christians become involved in Eastern practices which serve to

---

[61] In Chapter 6 of *God, Zen, and the Intuition of Being*, Jim Arraj develops a Thomistic understanding of the type of knowledge that results from the elimination of mental activity. He calls this knowledge through connaturality, and even suggests koans based on St. Thomas' philosophical insights.

[62] Buddhist meditation seems to place the strongest emphasis on this aspect of meditation. Indeed, nirvana might be understood as the development of this state of desirelessness. Consider, also, the line from the *Tao te Ching*, no. 1, which reads: "Ever desireless, one can see the mystery." Then there is St. John of the Cross' famous lines: "In order to arrive at being everything, desire to be nothing. In order to arrive at knowing everything, desire to know nothing." *Ascent of Mount Carmel.*

[63] In *God, Zen, and the Intuition of Being*, page 56, Jim Arraj calls this an experience of absolute self, and he quotes Jacques Maritain, who calls it an experience of "the soul's own substantial existence." Maritain and Arraj are both reflecting on the nature of the Ego-less experience using a Thomistic approach.

de-construct the Ego, spiritual directors will need to better understand how to help directees deal with the short and long-term consequences of these experiences.[64]

What ought to be abundantly clear from the above is that it is entirely possible to come to a direct experience of Self quite apart from any theistic context. God would be present in this experience, for God is immanent in Self. Nevertheless, God would not necessarily be known as a personal loving presence—as with the ecstasy of the religious contemplative (which is known in hindsight). Instead, the consciousness of Self would prevail, in all its cosmic, transcendent, holistic, and social splendor as a simple state of awareness prior to any movement of the will or intellect. All that one knows about oneself in this state is "that I am." As soon as the question, "but who am I?" comes along, the development of Ego as personal, defined consciousness begins to unfold once again, only now in a less rigid and illusory manner.

The direct experience of Self in a non-theistic context is how I understand Zen enlightenment, and some forms of yogic samadhi. Jim Arraj has described this as a *metaphysical mysticism*, rather than a religious mysticism in which God would be more explicitly known in the Self-God experience.[65] As Christianity continues to deepen its encounter with the religions of the far East, spiritual directors will need to better understand the nature of this experience and its potential value to directees. From the above, it should be obvious that the Self-God experience that one comes to through Zen, for example, is both similar to and different from the unitive experiences of Christian contemplatives. If these differences can be acknowledged and kept in perspective, then there is no reason whatsoever to discourage a directee from pursuing an Eastern pathway. The

---

[64] Gerald May has addressed this topic from several angles in his superb work on the spiritual life, *Will and Spirit: A Contemplative Psychology*. My own book, *Kundalini Energy and Christian Spirituality,* deals with the issue of energy and contemplative spirituality.

[65] *God, Zen and the Intuition of Being*, chapter 7.

Ego-God relationship should not be neglected, however, and only directees with a firm grounding in their own tradition should pursue such experiences. Beyond these two considerations, there is little justification for discouraging a directee from undertaking an Eastern practice to come to the knowledge of Self in God.

Throughout this discussion on facilitating knowledge of the Self-God union, we have been more concerned with coming to the direct experience of Self, rather than addressing the issue of facilitating a deepening union between Self and God—as between Ego and God. Whether anything can be done to affect the manner of union between Self and God is an interesting question, but one which we shall reflect on here only briefly. On the one hand, we have already affirmed the presence of a natural, or existential union between God and Self. We have also suggested that Self is non-intentional, which would seem to mitigate against deepening union between God and Self. Nevertheless, the Incarnation has established a new relationship between humanity and God. Three possible relationships between Christ and Self suggest themselves:

1. Because of the fundamental unity of the human species, we can minimally affirm that the consciousness of Christ is present in Self, and to awaken to Self is to experience something of his consciousness, even if this is not recognized. In this situation, it is possible that the Ego-Christ relationship effects a transformation at the level of Self through grace. As the Ego becomes increasingly identified with Christ, its ground in Self becomes correspondingly transformed into the consciousness of Christ. If this is the case, then a transformation in the Self-God union can be effected through the Ego-God relationship. What is suggested here is a spirituality of "becoming Christ" through grace—a very familiar paradigm for most Christians.

2. It may well be, however, that in "becoming sin" through empathic love, Christ became completely identified with all individuals, and thus bonded completely with the human condition as Self. By rising from the dead and ascending to

heaven, he would have thus taken Self into his own consciousness, in which case he would not be merely present in Self as another human being, but henceforth present to the human race *as Self*. Christ as Self: the interface between the human and divine! If this is the truth, then Ego is an individual expression of Christ, and the phrase, "What you do to one another, you do to me" takes on new poignancy.[66]

3. This possibility would be the same as no. 2, but would be applied only to baptized Christians, rather than to the whole human race. St. Paul suggests this when he writes, "You have been buried with him, when you were baptized; and by baptism, too, you have been raised up with him through your belief in the power of God who raised him from the dead. . . because you have died, the life you now have is hidden with Christ in God.

---

[66] In *Spiritual Development: An Interdisciplinary Approach*, Daniel Helminiak seems to concur with this particular Christology.

"To say that Christianity discloses a further dimension of human reality, the process of divinization, is not to suggest that Christian belief actualizes that further dimension. That is, one need not be Christian to participate in the divine fulfillment effected by God in Christ. . . what Christ effected in some way touches every person born into the human family, whether each of aware of Christ or not. . . The line between those who are in Christ and those who are not coincides with the line that divides the good from the wicked. The parable of the sheep and the goats says as much. Christian belief and baptism are not the telling issue. Human authenticity is. . . Granted that a person is authentic, seeking honestly to know and do what is right and good, holiness as relationship with God and divinization as participation in Christ both follow automatically. (pp. 166-167)"

Far from suggesting that Christian faith is irrelevant, however, Helminiak adds:

"Where Christianity is authentic, as with theism, it helps the believer to live authentically. . . Moreover, since the Christian believer not only lives a life in Christ but also knows and willingly embraces that life in Christ, he or she may attain a "higher degree of being" of that life in Christ. (p. 168)."

This "higher degree of being" is not a consequence of a transformation at the level of Self, but of a willing cooperation by Ego which Christian revelation and grace makes possible. The transformation effected is on the level of Ego, not Self.

But when Christ is revealed—and he is your life—you too will be revealed in all your glory with him (Col. 2: 12, 3: 3-4)."[67]

In any case, the spiritual work called for is the same, only one's understanding of grace and transformation is shifted from a perspective of "becoming Christ" to "realizing the Christ 'that I am.'" In the context of this present discussion on facilitating the Self-God union, the first Christology would tend to de-emphasize direct experience of Self, while the second and third would strongly emphasize this—especially for the baptized. My own sympathies are more with the first Christology, but further reflection on the many implications of this view would take us too far afield from the primary focus of this work. Nevertheless, the relationship between theology and spiritual practice ought to be obvious from this brief digression.

Ego-Self-God Union

From the foregoing, we have recognized three types of unitive experiences: Ego-God, Ego-Self, and Self-God. Facilitating the Ego- Self-God union would not entail doing anything different from what has been described above, only keeping it all in balance somehow. For example, it would be possible to become so focused on exploring the Self-God level that the Ego-God and Ego-Self experiences could become neglected. The consequence, in this case, would be lack of Egoic integration—possibly even psychological imbalances of some kind. Similarly,

---

[67] Writing on baptism in their *Dictionary of Theology*, Karl Rahner and Herbert Vorgrimler state that "Since only baptism bestows rebirth into the new life in Christ, this same life cannot in principle be had without baptism." In their section on Baptism of Desire, however, they note that "whoever is inculpably unaware of Christ's Gospel and the Church, but honestly seeks God and obeys his or her conscience, can attain to eternal salvation." The *Vatican II Dogmatic Constitution on the Church*, no. 16, makes the same point, seemingly concurring with Helminiak's reflections in footnote no. 66. Rahner, Vorgrimler, and the Bishops of Vatican II apply the concept of Baptism of Desire, and its "morality of authenticity," only to those who have not heard the Gospel, or who have rejected the Gospel because of bad example. There is no suggestion in any of this that the Church has become somehow irrelevant to God's plan for saving the human race.

an overemphasis on the Ego-God relationship could lead to a lack of psychological self-knowledge, while focusing too much on Ego-Self could result in the loss of a sense of God's transcendence and mystery.

Traditionally, Christian spirituality has attempted to keep these pieces in balance by encouraging the development of contemplative experience. One began with the Ego-God relationship, which was nourished by the Church's teachings and Sacraments, and developed in the context of active, interpersonal prayer. In time, this prayer became radically simplified, and one became content to simply rest in a general, loving awareness of God's presence. This resting in God, which is the essence of contemplative prayer, was accompanied by healings in the unconscious level of the psyche, which enabled a closer correspondence between Ego and Self. During periods of very deep prayer, Egoic consciousness might even be transcended for awhile, with the Self-God union predominating—as has been described in the above section. In the context of the deepening Ego- God relationship, then, the Ego-Self union was developed, and the Self-God union became manifest at times.

Although this approach might seem "tried and true" and requiring no adjustments, there are at least two very good reasons why it is sometimes woefully inadequate. The first is that many directees have suffered considerable psychological abuse, which has created severe distortions in the Ego-Self relationship. While it is obvious that they can experience some relief and healing from prayer, it may well be that their progress in prayer is limited by the very defenses and coping mechanisms they have developed to minimize their experience of pain. Without some kind of psychological intervention to help unravel distortions in the Ego-Self relationship, progress in the Ego- God relationship will be impeded. We need only to listen to the experiences of many who have availed themselves of such healing to learn how much this has contributed to their growth in prayer. Spiritual directors would do well to refer directees to the appropriate counseling professional when the need arises—as, indeed, most who practice this ministry are already doing.

The second objection to over-emphasizing the Ego-God relationship as the key to developing the Ego-Self-God union is that, for reasons known to God alone, many very good people with sincere intent do not come to experience contemplative prayer. Neither do they continue to enjoy more active and discursive forms of prayer. After making a good start in the spiritual life, they come to a place of aridity, and the desert just never seems to bloom into the oases described by contemplatives and mystics. Sometimes, this situation goes on and on for years, with the directee persisting in faith, prayer, and service, but seeming to be getting nowhere at all. It is fine and well for the director to say that even though it seems that things aren't happening, they really are—just at a level the directee cannot experience, for now. One can provide this kind of encouragement for only so long, however.

For those who do not seem to be experiencing contemplation, or who seem to be "stuck" because of psychological problems, it may be necessary to develop the Ego-Self-God union "piecemeal," or in stages. In addition to the Ego-God relationship, the Ego-Self and Self-God relationships can also be developed using some of the approaches and resources described in the previous sections. For example, one could work on the Ego-Self relationship through psychological counseling, dream work, the Enneagram, or Jung's psychological types. Perhaps a little progress in this direction will clear away some of the obstacles to receiving contemplative graces. At any rate, this area of development has been well explored during this century, and there are many directors who already know how to help a directee move in this direction and integrate their discoveries in the Ego-God relationship.

This is not the case with the Self-God relationship, however. At this time in Christian history, the value of investigating this experience is still somewhat controversial. In the absence of ecstatic contemplative experiences, the only "ways" to the Self-

God experience seem to be some of the more impersonal methods of Eastern religions. This raises theological questions for many directors, who may not be very familiar with the religion of the far East. Then there are practical concerns, such as the energy upheavals and psychic experiences which sometimes accompany investigations into this realm of the deep. Although we are still learning how to respond to these theological, anthropological and pastoral issues, there are a few promising signs which suggest that direct knowledge of the Self-God relationship can be a boon to the Christian life. Most encouraging of all are the experiences of those Christians who have investigated this experience, and learned to integrate it. They are not many in number, but they do give testimony to the compatibility between Christian faith and Eastern experiences. Some of these pioneers are spiritual directors, but, on the whole, most Christian spiritual directors are probably unfamiliar with these experiences.

The piece-meal approach to developing the Ego-Self-God relationship is, then, a relatively new possibility in Christian spirituality. How to proceed on such a journey without allowing one of the pieces to overshadow the others is a real challenge, but one that is not insurmountable. The key, I believe, is to maintain the Ego-God relationship while developing the other two pieces. If this primary focus is lost, then the directee runs the risk of falling into an Eastern pathway, or psychological self-salvation, or, most likely, some kind of syncretism. If the Ego-God relationship is maintained by at least a purely intellectual faith, however, this will provide an over-arching Christian context for integrating the other pieces of spiritual development. In the long run, all the pieces will find a way to fit together, and it will be these intellectual convictions which provide the "form," as it were, in which they interact.

Whether one travels the contemplative route or the piecemeal route, the fruit of the Ego-Self-God relationship is the ability to abide in the worlds of unity and duality. The mystery of the one and the many takes us back to the beginning of Part I, and our reflections on essence and existence. To over-emphasize essence is duality; to over-emphasize Existence is monistic. At every moment and in every place, everything created is both one in God, and simultaneously distinct from God. This is the truth affirmed through the philosophical reflections of St. Thomas Aquinas. As the Ego-Self- God relationship is developed and integrated, this truth is also known experientially. Only then do we know what it means to live life to the full.

References Cited in Footnotes

Angels (and Demons): What Do We Really Know About Them? by Peter Kreft. Ignatius Press. San Francisco, CA. 1995.

Ascent of Mount Carmel, in *The Collected Works of St. John of the Cross.* ICS Publications. Washington, D.C. 1991.

Being in Love: The Practice of Christian Prayer, by William Johnston, S.J. Fount (Harper-Collins). London. 1988.

Co-Dependence: Misunderstood, Mistreated, by Anne Wilson Schaef. Winston Press. Minneapolis, MN. 1986.

Dark Night of the Soul, by St. John of the Cross (E. Allison Peers translation). Doubleday/Image. Garden City, NY. 1959.

Dictionary of Theology, by Karl Rahner and Herbert Vorgrimler. Crossroads Publ. New York. 1981.

Ego Development, by Jane Loevinger. Jossey-Bass Publ. San Fran- cisco, CA. 1977.

Fully Human, Fully Alive: A New Life Through a New Vision, by John Powell, S.J. Tabor Publ. Allen, TX. 1976.

God, Zen and the Intuition of Being, by James Arraj. Inner Growth Books. Chiloquin, OR. 1988.

Handbook for Spiritual Growth: A Guide for Catholics, by Philip St. Romain. Liguori Publ. Liguori, MO. 1993.

Invitation to Love: The Way of Christian Contemplation, by Thomas Keating, O.C.S.O. Element. Rockport, MA. 1992.

Journal of Transpersonal Psychology, Vol. 27 (1995): No. 1.

Jungian and Catholic? The Promises and Problems of the Jungian- Christian Dialogue, by James Arraj. Inner Growth Books. Chiloquin, OR. 1991..

Kundalini Energy and Christian Spirituality, by Philip St. Romain. Crossroads Publ. New York. 1991.

Kundalini, Evolution and Enlightenment, by John White (ed.). Paragon House. New York. 1990.

Lessons in Loving: Developing Relationship Skills, by Philip St. Romain. Liguori Publ. Liguori, MO. 1988.

Man and His Symbols, by Carl G. Jung (ed.). Doubleday & Co. Garden City, NY. 1964.

Mysticism, Metaphysics and Maritain: On the Road to the Spiritual Unconscious, by James Arraj. Inner Growth Books. Chiloquin, OR. 1993.

Saccidananda: A Christian Approach to Advaitic Experience, by Swami Abishiktananda. I.S.P.C.K. Kashmere Gate. Delhi, India.

Search for the Meaning of Life: Essays and Reflections on the Mystical Experience, by Willigis Jaeger. Triumph Books. Liguori, MO. 1995.

Spiritual Development: An Interdisciplinary Approach, by Daniel Helminiak. Loyola University Press. Chicago, IL. 1987.

The Complete, Illustrated Book of Yoga, by Swami Vishnu-devananda. Harmony Books. New York. 1960/88.

The Fires of Desire: Erotic Energies and the Spiritual Quest, by Fredrica R. Halligan and John J. Shea (ed.). Crossroad Publ. New York. 1992.

The Imitation of Christ, by Thomas a Kempis. Image/Doubleday. Garden City, NY. 1955 edition.

The Inner Nature of Faith: A Mysterious Knowledge Coming Through the Heart, by James Arraj. Inner Growth Books. Chiloquin, OR. 1988.

The Perennial Philosophy, by Aldous Huxley. Harper & Row, Publ. San Francisco. 1945.

The Portable Jung, by Joseph Campbell (ed.). Viking/Penguin Books. New York. 1971.

The Summa Theologia, by St. Thomas Aquinas. Benziger Br., Inc. New York. 1947.

The Tao te Ching, by Lao Tsu, translated by Gia-Fu Feng and Jane English. Vintage Books. New York. 1972.

The Theology of Christian Perfection, by Antonio Royo, O.P. and Jordan Aumann, O.P. Priory Press. Dubuque, IA. 1962.

The Twelve Steps, A Spiritual Journey: A Working Guide for Healing Damaged Emotions. RPI Publ. San Diego, CA. 1994.

Tracking the Elusive Human (Vol. I), by James and Tyra Arraj. Inner Growth Books. Chiloquin, OR. 1988.

Transpersonal Psychotherapies, ed. by Seymour Boorstein, M.D. JTP Books. Stanford, CA. 1991.

Twelve Steps To Spiritual Wholeness: A Christian Pathway, by Philip St. Romain. Liguori Publ. Liguori, MO. 1992.

Vatican Council II: The Conciliar and Post-Conciliar Documents, ed. by Austin Flannery, O.P. Costello Publ. Northport, NY. 1981.

Will and Spirit: A Contemplative Psychology, by Gerald G. May, M.D. Harper & Row Publ. San Francisco, CA. 1982.

Will the Real Me Please Stand Up: 25 Guidelines for Good Communication, by John Powell, S.J. and Loretta Brady, M.S.W. Tabor Publ. Allen, TX. 1985.

Zen and the Birds of Appetite, by Thomas Merton. New Direction Publ. New York. 1968.

Zen Catholicism, by Dom Aelred Graham. Crossroad Publ. New York. 1963/94.

Figure One

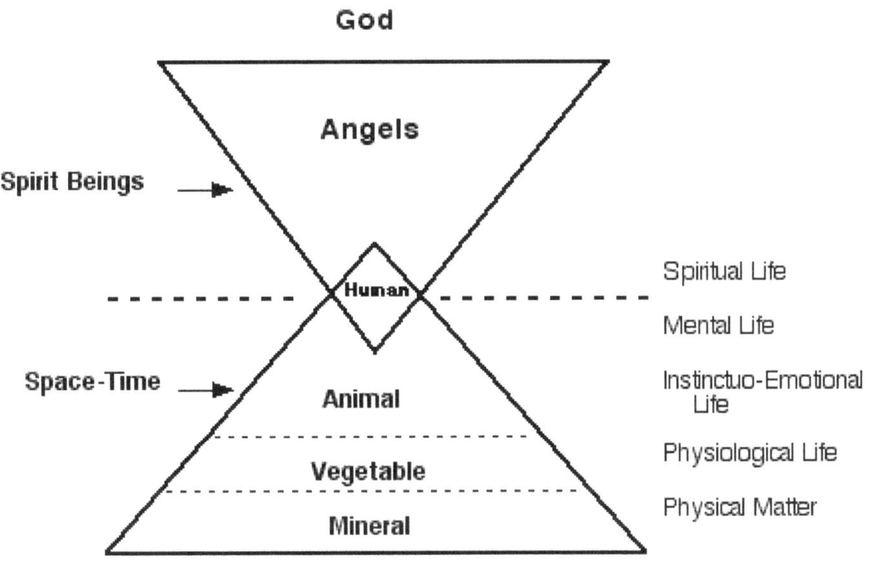

God and Creation
(God in all the Empty Spaces)

Adapted from *Angels (and Demons)*, by Peter Kreft

God, Self and Ego
Discerning "Who's Who" on the Spiritual Journey

Abstract

The ministry of spiritual direction has as its primary goal a deepening of the experience of union between the directee and God. Generally, the director helps to facilitate the Spirit-directee relationship by listening to and validating experiences, challenging unreasonable beliefs and attachments, recommending prayer exercises and reading materials, and co-discerning the leadings of the Spirit. In all of these roles, however, the director's own assumptions about human nature and divine union figure significantly. Some directors, for example, consider almost every kind of Ego-transcending experience to be an encounter with God. Others recognize a variety of psychological and unitive experiences. The purpose of this doctoral project is to establish terminology and criteria pertaining to the experiences of God, Self, and Ego and the manner in which these entities participate in union with each other.

A brief perusal of the literature will reveal many inconsistencies in the manner in which the terms God, Self, and Ego are used. In this project, I shall attempt to utilize experiential definitions for each, and relate these to the works of other writers. For purposes of clarifying the relationships between these experiences, I shall make use of the metaphysical insights of St. Thomas Aquinas and his explicators, whose writings have served Christianity very well for several centuries.

Thomism recognizes two aspects to reality: existence and essence. Existence refers to the fact that something is; essence refers to what something is. When applied to the realm of human interiority, these two aspects of reality correspond to the experiences that I am and who I am, respectively. Most definitions of Self seem to pertain to the the realm of existence, and the most common use of the term Ego is in relation to essence. Self is that I am, and Ego is what or who I am. The relationship between Self and Ego can be deduced from these affirmations: Self is the more basic entity—human consciousness—and Ego is an individual manifestation of Self. In this view, then, Ego and Self are not metaphysically opposed, and a harmonious union between the two is the natural order of things. Ego is the intentional aspect of Self, and Self is the subjective aspect of Ego.

The relationship between Self and God is analogous to the Ego-Self relationship. Self is not God, but neither is it separate from God. Self exists as Self because God gives it existence as such, and this very fact implies something of a natural, or existential union between God and Self. God is immanent in Self, and Self exists in God.

The view of human nature described by Thomists also tells us something about its interior attitudes. The soul is essentially spiritual, but it incorporates the dimensions of animal, vegetable (physiological), and inanimate being. Hence, Self is open to transcendence, open to the cosmos, and present in every level of human existence. Self is also inherently relational since it is possessed by each individual, but more fully manifest in community. To the extent that the Ego adopts these basic "attitudes" of Self, it will be in authentic relationship with God, other people, the cosmos, and Self.

Considering the relationship between God, Self, and Ego together, then, one can conclude that no disharmony is implied in the nature of the relationship between these entities. The Self which Ego manifests is God's "habitat" in each person. To the extent that the Ego is in a harmonious relationship with Self, it is also in harmony with God, and knows something of the presence of God in Self. Thus the dignity of Ego is affirmed in this view.

The universal human experience is that disharmony does exist in the human psyche. The Ego-Self-God alignment is disordered, and the overwhelming testimony of the world religions is that non-love is the reason for this disease. In response to developing in a climate of non-love, the Ego's desires becomes skewed in the interest of minimizing pain and maximizing personal survival. A whole system of dysfunctional behavioral conditioning develops, all premised on the convictions that the individual is unworthy, unlovable, unacceptable, and incapable. This system of conditioning is the false self. It has no metaphysical reality as such, but because it functions more or less autonomously—frequently against the better judgment of the Ego—it feels as though it has a life of its own. This false self conditioning, not the Ego, is the primary obstacle to the experience of union with God. Understanding the false self-Ego- Self relationships is thus of primary importance in facilitating ongoing union with God, the goal of spiritual direction.

Given these brief descriptions of false self, Ego, Self, and God, several different unitive experiences can be acknowledged:

1. *False self-Ego union.* Even though the false self has no substantial nature, its mode of operation is Egoic. This is one reason why many have written about the sinful nature of the Ego, and bemoaned the irresponsibility of the Ego. The problem is the false self infection of Ego, however, and not the fact of the Ego's existence. This understanding has many implications for spiritual practice.

2. *Ego-Self union.* This is a good and natural relationship, which Jungian psychology has investigated extensively. The development of this union is the project Jung called individuation. It can also be developed through a variety of other disciplines which emphasize authenticity in speech, thought, and behavior.

3. *Self-God union.* If Ego's desires could be extinguished, along with the intellectual convictions which support them, then the "suchness" of Self and its union with God and creation could be experienced directly and non-reflectively. God would not be known as relational partner, however, but would be implicit

in the Self and in creation and known as Void, or Emptiness. Some forms of Eastern mysticism seem to emphasize this union.

4. *Ego-God union.* A wide variety of possibilities exist, here. In general, God is considered as an-Other Being with Whom the Ego relates through the medium of ideas, concepts, feelings, desires, images and symbols. God can and often does communicate with the Ego in this manner, as the Judeo-Christian tradition of revelation emphasizes. Because the life of the Ego is under the sway of the false self, however, its relationship with God can be distorted in many ways.

5. *Ego-Self-God union.* This is contemplative union as understood in the Catholic mystical tradition. Here, the Ego relates to God intellectually and affectively, as described above, but also experiences God through the unconscious realm of the psyche, of which the Self is central. Thus does the Ego develop its connection with Self in the context of its relationship with God. During ecstatic experiences, the Ego may be lost for awhile, with the Self-God union predominating, but eventually the Ego returns to integrate the ecstatic experience consciously and in the overall lifestyle. The Ego-Self-God union, then, is both mystical and individuating.

Having established terminology and criteria for understanding different kinds of unitive experiences as sketched above, the project concludes by drawing out the practical implications for spiritual directors.

www.ingramcontent.com/pod-product-compliance
Ingram Content Group UK Ltd.
Pitfield, Milton Keynes, MK11 3LW, UK
UKHW041915190726
13854UKWH00003B/1264